POETRY

Essential Literary Genres

BY JENNIFER JOLINE ANDERSON

Essential Library

An Imprint of Abdo Publishing | abdopublishing.com

ABDOPUBLISHING.COM

Published by Abdo Publishing, a division of ABDO, PO Box 398166, Minneapolis, Minnesota
55439. Copyright © 2017 by Abdo Consulting Group, Inc. International copyrights
reserved in all countries. No part of this book may be reproduced in any form without
written permission from the publisher. Essential Library™ is a trademark and logo of Abdo
Publishing.

Printed in the United States of America, North Mankato, Minnesota
102016
012017

Interior Photos: Georgios Kollidas/Shutterstock Images, 11; Stocksnapper/Shutterstock
Images, 12; Marice Cohn Band/KRT/Newscom, 15; Shutterstock Images, 17, 19, 26, 43,
44–45, 66–67, 75, 85; Kitja Kitja/Shutterstock Images, 22–23; Remo Nassi/AP Images,
28; Pictorial Press Ltd/Alamy, 34–35; Everett - Art/Shutterstock Images, 41; Vincent
Voigt/iStockphoto, 45; iStockphoto, 51; IanDagnall Computing/Alamy, 57; Marc Bruxelle/
Shutterstock Images, 59; Robsonphoto/Shutterstock Images, 64; Tommy Brison/Shutterstock
Images, 69; Sogno Lucido/Shutterstock Images, 71; Blend Images/Shutterstock Images, 73;
DPA Picture Alliance/Alamy, 81; Bettmann/Getty Images, 82; Sam Camp/iStockphoto, 86;
Posonskyi Andrey/Shutterstock Images, 89; AP Images, 90–91; Universal History Archive/
Getty Images, 96

Editor: Arnold Ringstad
Series Designer: Maggie Villaume

PUBLISHER'S CATALOGING-IN-PUBLICATION DATA

Names: Anderson, Jennifer Joline, author.
Title: Poetry / by Jennifer Joline Anderson.
Description: Minneapolis, MN : Abdo Publishing, 2017. | Series: Essential
    literary genres | Includes bibliographical references and index.
Identifiers: LCCN 2016945208 | ISBN 9781680783827 (lib. bdg.) |
    ISBN 9781680797350 (ebook)
Subjects: LCSH: Literature--Juvenile literature. | Literary form--Juvenile
    literature.
Classification: DDC 809--dc23
LC record available at http://lccn.loc.gov/2016945208

CONTENTS

INTRODUCTION TO
LITERARY GENRES

Why do we read and write literature? Telling stories is an integral part of being human, a universal experience across history and cultures. Literature as we know it today is the written form of these stories and ideas. Writing allows authors to take their readers on a journey that crosses the boundaries of space and time. Literature allows us to understand the experiences of others and express experiences of our own.

What Is a Genre?

A genre is a specific category, or type, of literature. Broad genres of literature include nonfiction, poetry, drama, and fiction. Smaller groupings include subject-based genres such as mystery, science fiction, romance, or fantasy. Literature can also be classified by its audience, such as young adult (YA) or children's, or its format, such as a graphic novel or picture book.

What Are Literary Theory and Criticism?

Literary theory gives us tools to help decode a text. On one level, we can examine the words and phrases the author uses so we can interpret or debate his or her message. We can ask questions about how the book's structure creates an effect on the reader, and whether this is the effect the author intended. We can analyze symbolism or themes in a work. We can dive deeper by asking how a work either supports or challenges society and its values or traditions.

You can look at these questions using different criticisms, or schools of thought. Each type of criticism asks you to look at the work from a different perspective. Perhaps you want to examine what the work says about the writer's life or the time period in which the work was created. Biographical or historical criticism considers these questions. Or perhaps you are interested in what the work says about the role of women or the structure of society. Feminist or Marxist theories seek to answer those types of questions.

How Do You Apply Literary Criticism?

You write an analysis when you use a literary or critical approach to examine and question a work. The theory you choose is a lens through which you can view the work, or a springboard for asking questions about the work. Applying a theory helps you think critically. You are free to question the work and make an assertion about it. If you choose to examine a work using racial criticism, for example, you may ask questions about how the work challenges or upholds racial structures in society. Or you may ask how a character's race affects his or her identity or development throughout the work.

Forming a Thesis

Form your questions and find answers in the work or other related materials. Then you can create a thesis. The thesis is the key point in your analysis. It is your argument about the work based on the school of thought you are using. For example, if you want to approach a work using feminist criticism, you could write the following thesis: The character of Margy in Sissy Johnson's *Margy Sings the Blues* uses her songwriting to subvert traditional gender roles.

HOW TO MAKE A THESIS STATEMENT

In an analysis, a thesis statement typically appears at the end of the introductory paragraph. It is usually only one sentence long and states the author's main idea.

Providing Evidence

Once you have formed a thesis, you must provide evidence to support it. Evidence will usually take the form of examples and quotations from the work itself, often including dialogue from a character. You may wish to address what others have written about the work. Quotes from these individuals may help support your claim. If you find any quotes or examples that contradict your thesis, you will need to create an argument against them. For instance: Many critics claim Margy's actions uphold traditional gender roles, even if her songs went against them. However, the novel's resolution proves Margy had the power to change society through her music.

HOW TO SUPPORT A THESIS STATEMENT

An analysis should include several arguments that support the thesis's claim. An argument is one or two sentences long and is supported by evidence from the work being discussed. Organize the arguments into paragraphs. These paragraphs make up the body of the analysis.

Concluding the Essay

After you have written several arguments and included evidence to support them, finish the essay with a conclusion. The conclusion restates the ideas from the

HOW TO CONCLUDE AN ESSAY

Begin your conclusion with a recap of the thesis and a brief summary of the most important or strongest arguments. Leave readers with a final thought that puts the essay in a larger context or considers its wider implications.

thesis and summarizes some of the main points from the essay. The conclusion's final thought often considers additional implications for the essay or gives the reader something to ponder further.

In This Book

In this book, you will read summaries of works, each followed by an analysis. Critical thinking sections will give you a chance to consider other theses and questions about the work. Did you agree with the author's analysis? What other questions are raised by the thesis and its arguments? You can also see other directions the author could have pursued to analyze the work. Then, in the Analyze It section in the final pages of this book, you will have an opportunity to create your own analysis paper.

The Genre of Poetry

Poetry is perhaps the oldest genre of literature. It appeared long before written language, as ancient storytellers shared ballads and epics by word of mouth.

Poetic techniques of rhyme, rhythm, and repetition made their tales pleasing to the ear and easier to remember.

In general, most poems share several features. Unlike prose, which is written in sentences and paragraphs, poetry is typically written in verse and arranged in lines and stanzas. Poetry relies on the sound and rhythm of words. Techniques such as rhythm, rhyme, alliteration, and assonance are used to create various effects of mood and tone. Poetry is also rich in figurative language such as metaphor and simile, and often contains vivid imagery.

Poetry packs a great deal of meaning into few words. Words are carefully chosen and may have a deeper significance that is revealed only after careful analysis. The syntax, or word order, may be arranged in unusual ways, making the meaning challenging to interpret. Even a short poem can benefit from a close, line-by-line reading. It may have numerous themes, or messages, waiting to be discovered.

LOOK FOR THE GUIDES

Throughout the chapters that analyze the works, thesis statements have been highlighted. The box next to the thesis helps explain what questions are being raised about the work. Supporting arguments have also been highlighted. The boxes next to the arguments help explain how these points support the thesis. The conclusions are also accompanied by explanatory boxes. Look for these guides throughout each analysis.

OVERVIEWS OF
SONNET 130 AND "LOVE SONG FOR LOVE SONGS"

The sonnet, a 14-line rhyming poem, has been a common form of poetry for hundreds of years. Sonnets originated in Italy and were popularized by the Italian Renaissance poet Francesco Petrarca, known in English as Petrarch, in the 1300s. The word *sonnet* comes from the Italian *sonetto,* meaning "a little song." True to the name, sonnets are short, musical lyrics that share the personal feelings of a speaker.

The sonnet spread to the rest of Europe during the Renaissance, reaching France, Spain, and Germany. In the 1500s, Sir Thomas Wyatt introduced the poetic form to England, and it quickly grew in popularity.

Petrarch was among the earliest major figures
in the Italian Renaissance.

Shakespeare is acclaimed as the greatest
English writer in history

Sonnets soon became among the most widespread types of poetry in the country. Innovators such as Sir Edmund Spenser and William Shakespeare adapted the style to their own liking, tweaking the structure and rhyme scheme, and their formats became widely known.

The most famous sonnets in the English language are those of Shakespeare, who wrote in the late 1500s and early 1600s. Shakespeare was a poet and playwright of the Elizabethan period. His plays and sonnets contributed to what is known as the Golden Age of English literature. Shakespeare's sonnets cover various themes, including loneliness and mortality, but the majority are love poems.

Sonnets have a strict pattern of rhythm and rhyme. Petrarchan, or Italian, sonnets contain an octave followed by an answering sestet. The rhyme scheme is *abbaabba*, then *cdcdcd* or *cdecde*. Shakespearean, or English, sonnets have three quatrains and a final couplet. The rhyme scheme is *abab cdcd efef gg*. The meter of an English sonnet is known as iambic pentameter. Each line of verse contains ten syllables, and every other syllable is stressed. This metrical pattern creates a smooth, flowing rhythm that can be heard when the poem is read aloud.

Both Italian and English sonnets are structured in the form of an argument. In a Petrarchan sonnet, the argument or problem is described in the octave, and the sestet contains an answer or solution. The turning point between the two parts is called the volta. In Shakespearean sonnets, the argument is presented in the first three quatrains. The turning point comes in the final couplet, which offers a surprising conclusion.

The following are two sonnets that share the theme of love. The first, Sonnet 130, was written by William Shakespeare sometime between 1593 and 1601. The second, "Love Song for Love Songs," was written by the poet Rafael Campo in 2012. Campo was born in New Jersey in 1964 to Cuban and Italian parents. A physician as well as a poet, he practices at Harvard Medical School. Campo is openly gay, and he writes about issues that affect gay, lesbian, and transgender people. In his poem, Campo echoes Shakespeare's famous sonnet both in its structure and theme.

Campo authored six collections of poetry by 2016.

SONNET 130
BY WILLIAM SHAKESPEARE

My mistress' eyes are nothing like the sun;

Coral is far more red than her lips' red;

If snow be white, why then her breasts are dun;

If hairs be wires, black wires grow on her head.

I have seen roses damasked, red and white,

But no such roses see I in her cheeks;

And in some perfumes is there more delight

Than in the breath that from my mistress reeks.

I love to hear her speak, yet well I know

That music hath a far more pleasing sound;

I grant I never saw a goddess go;

My mistress when she walks treads on the ground.

And yet, by heaven, I think my love as rare

As any she belied with false compare.[1]

Shakespeare contrasts his subject's appearance with objects traditionally seen as beautiful, such as roses.

LOVE SONG FOR LOVE SONGS
BY RAFAEL CAMPO

A golden age of love songs and we still

can't get it right. Does your kiss really taste

like butter cream? To me, the moon's bright face

was neither like a pizza pie nor full;

the Beguine began, but my eyelid twitched.

"No more I love you's," someone else assured

us, pouring out her heart, in love (of course)—

what bothers me the most is that high-pitched,

undone whine of "Why am I so alone?"

Such rueful misery is closer to

the truth, but once you turn the lamp down low,

you must admit that he is still the one,

and baby, baby he makes you so dumb

you sing in the shower at the top of your lungs.[2]

Campo dismisses the objects of comparison, such as the moon, that are often seen in popular love songs.

Poetic Technique

Sonnet 130 is a classic Shakespearean sonnet. It can be broken down into three quatrains and a final couplet, with the rhyme scheme *abab cdcd efef gg*. Campo's poem is also written in sonnet form but with an alternate rhyme scheme: *abba cddc effe gg*. Most are not true rhymes, but slant or eye rhymes created by a similar sound or spelling, as in *still/full*, *dumb/lungs*, and *alone/one*.

Both poems are written in iambic pentameter, with ten syllables and approximately five beats per line. Shakespeare's lines have a steady beat with the stress falling on approximately every other syllable: "My *mis* | tress' *eyes* | are *no* | thing *like* | the *sun*." The rhythm in Campo's poem is more irregular, following the cadence of actual speech. In Shakespeare's sonnet, the lines are end-stopped. Each line contains a complete thought. But in Campo's poem, the thoughts run from line to line. This technique, known as enjambment, gives the poem a more modern, less formal style.

As is typical of sonnets, both poems are written as an argument followed by a surprising or contradictory conclusion. Shakespeare seems to be insulting his mistress throughout the poem. But the final couplet reveals that he actually thinks she is very special, and his true aim is to make fun of the exaggerated compliments many poets use to describe women. Campo expresses a cynical attitude toward love songs—and love in general—throughout the first eight lines of his poem. A turning point comes in line 9, as the speaker considers the alternative to love: loneliness. In the final couplet, he abandons his skeptical view and admits he loves love as much as anyone else.

RHETORICAL ANALYSIS OF LOVE SONNETS

Rhetorical analysis is a method of examining literature that involves studying how an author uses particular words and phrases to influence the reader. This critical lens can be used to look at the relationship between the work's message and the form in which the author is choosing to convey it. Shakespeare's Sonnet 130 and Campo's "Love Song for Love Songs" were written more than 400 years apart, yet they are similar in their form and message. A comparison of their forms reveals how both poems use poetic

Both Shakespeare and Campo use the sonnet to examine the theme of love.

THESIS STATEMENT

ARGUMENT ONE

techniques to advance a theme. While Shakespeare creates a parody of love poems in the Golden Age of English literature, Campo's poem does the same for the lyrics from a "golden age" of American songwriting. A rhetorical analysis of Sonnet 130 and "Love Song for Love Songs" reveals that each poet uses the conventional form of the sonnet, along with contemporary allusions, to critique the love songs of his time while still convincing the reader that love itself can be authentic and worthwhile.

Both poems adhere to the formal characteristics of the sonnet. The quatrains present an idea, question, or problem, and the final couplet presents a surprising answer. Sonnet 130 is a classic Shakespearean

sonnet, with the rhyme scheme *abab cdcd efef gg*.
Campo's poem is also written in sonnet form, but with
an alternate rhyme scheme: *abba cddc effe gg*. Many
of Campo's rhymes are not true rhymes. Instead, he
uses slant rhymes, which employ similar sounds, or
eye rhymes, which employ similar spellings. Examples
of these include *still/full* and *alone/one*. Both poems
are written in iambic pentameter, although Campo's
rhythm is more irregular. While Shakespeare's lines
are end-stopped, Campo's use of enjambment gives his
poem a more modern, free-flowing style suitable to his
subject: popular music.

While written in a formal
style, Shakespeare's Sonnet
130 is a lighthearted spoof
of the love sonnets of his
day. The word *sonnet* means
"a little song," and true
to the name, the sonnet
was the pop song of the
Renaissance, with lyrics just
as corny as those on the radio today. Shakespeare's poem
alludes to some of the many clichés used by his fellow
sonneteers: a beautiful woman had eyes "like the sun,"

lips "red as coral," and breasts as "white as snow." Blonde hair was likened to the golden wire used in jewelry, and a woman's breath was like perfume. Shakespeare reverses these clichés, exaggerating for comic effect. His mistress's eyes are "nothing like the sun," her hair is like "black wires," and her breath actually "reeks."

Although his description in the first three quatrains may sound insulting, the final couplet contradicts that idea. The speaker says he believes his beloved is just as special as any other woman who has been "belied," or misrepresented, by "false compare." The true message of the poem is to expose how ridiculous these false comparisons are when describing a real woman. Ironically, even as Shakespeare makes fun of romantic comparisons, he reveals he is a romantic too when he admits to thinking his love is "rare." He truly loves his mistress, and this is a sincere love poem.

As did Shakespeare before him, Campo pokes fun at the lyrics of popular songs. Allusions to contemporary love songs are interwoven throughout the poem: a moon "like a pizza pie" from the Dean Martin hit "That's Amore"; Cole Porter's love song "Begin the Beguine"; and the 1990s ballad "No More I Love Yous." Toward the end of the poem, Campo cheekily alludes to the blues tune "Turn the Lamp Down Low," by Muddy Waters, and the 1976 soft-rock love song "Still the One." The poem's speaker expresses a cynical attitude toward these lyrics, implying they

ARGUMENT FOUR

In argument four, the author compares Campo's poem to Shakespeare's, showing how both function as parodies: "As did Shakespeare before him, Campo pokes fun at the lyrics of popular songs."

ARGUMENT FIVE

The author continues the comparison, describing evidence of sonnet structure in Campo's poem: "In keeping with sonnet form, the final lines of the poem contain a turn, or volta, marked by a dramatic change in tone."

are unrealistic and that love is actually a quite miserable experience.

In keeping with sonnet form, the final lines of the poem contain a turn, or volta, marked by a dramatic change in tone. Having criticized love songs as irritatingly absurd, the speaker contemplates the alternative to love—being alone—and

Cole Porter was one of Broadway's most successful writers of music and lyrics from the 1920s to the 1950s.

rejects it. In the final couplet, he confesses he cannot resist them: "once you turn the lamp down low, / you must admit that he is still the one, / and baby, baby, he makes you so dumb / you sing in the shower at the top of your lungs" (11–14). The humorous image of a love-struck person singing dumb songs in the shower conveys the true message of the poem. The romantic view of love may be unrealistic and even ridiculous, but people often fall for it anyway.

The sonnet structure helps shape the message of both poems, as the reader is led through the argument to a surprising conclusion. Shakespeare seems to be insulting his mistress throughout the poem, but the final couplet reveals that he actually thinks she is very special, and his true aim is to make fun of the exaggerated compliments many poets use to describe women. Campo expresses a cynical attitude toward love songs—and love in general—throughout the first eight lines of his poem. A turning point comes in line 9, as he

ARGUMENT SIX

In the final argument, the author summarizes how the sonnet form helps deliver the message of each poem: "The sonnet structure helps shape the message of both poems, as the reader is led through the argument to a surprising conclusion."

abandons his skeptical view and admits he loves love as much as anyone else.

Shakespeare's and Campo's poems, written centuries apart, are love songs that make fun of love songs. Both poems use the age-old form of the sonnet to playfully critique the ridiculous, and yet timeless, clichés of romantic love, which were as common in Shakespeare's time as they are today. Although both poets mockingly reject the flowery language of love poetry and song, both ultimately embrace a romantic view of love.

CONCLUSION

The last paragraph of the essay is the conclusion. The author summarizes how the poems' structure and technique help convey a message about romantic love.

THINKING
CRITICALLY

Now it's your turn to assess the essay. Consider these questions:

1. Do you think the author did a good job of explaining how the sonnet form helped enhance the theme in each poem? Were there any points she could have explained more clearly?

2. Do you agree with the author that both poems convey a positive message about love? What other messages or themes could readers find in the poems?

3. Did reading this essay about the sonnets change your opinion about love poetry and love songs? Do you tend to be cynical about them?

OTHER
APPROACHES

The essay you have just read analyzes how two poets used the structure of a sonnet to create a parody, or critique, of the conventions of love poetry. Here are two additional approaches. One examines how the poems reflect an evolution of the sonnet form over time. The other examines how Campo handles gender in his poem.

The Sonnet Form from Petrarch to Today

The sonnet form has a long history, dating back to the Italian Renaissance with the poems of Petrarch. A comparison of Shakespeare's sonnets to Petrarchan sonnets reveals key changes in form and style to make the form more suitable to the English, rather than Italian, language. Contemporary sonnets are less strict in form, employing slant rhyme and enjambment. A thesis statement examining the poems from this angle might be, Shakespeare's and Campo's poems demonstrate the evolution of the sonnet to reflect contemporary taste in poetry.

Gender Criticism

In his poem "Love Song for Love Songs," Campo creates the image of someone newly in love: "you must admit that he is still the one, / and baby, baby he makes you so dumb / you sing in the shower at the top of your lungs." Campo is openly gay, and his preference is to date men, not women. The use of the word *he* in these lines may be a clue that he was thinking of a particular time when he fell in love with a man. However, Campo leaves the lines open to interpretation. The reader is free to imagine the person in the shower as male, female, or transgender, and the love relationship as being straight or gay. His poem, then, can be read as a celebration of romantic love between partners of any gender. A thesis statement that examines the poem from this angle might be: Campo's poem "Love Song for Love Songs" celebrates romantic love regardless of sexual orientation.

4

AN OVERVIEW OF "MY LAST DUCHESS"

English poet and playwright Robert Browning (1812–1889) is one of the most beloved poets of the Victorian Era (1837–1901), the period when Queen Victoria ruled the United Kingdom. His wife, Elizabeth Barrett Browning, was also a renowned poet. Browning was especially known for his dramatic monologues.

A dramatic monologue is usually directed at another character who remains silent. The speaker in this type of poem is not the poet but an invented character, as in a drama or play. Throughout the monologue, the

Browning wrote many poems over a career that lasted more than 50 years.

speaker reveals his or her personality and motivations to the reader.

Browning's 1842 poem "My Last Duchess" is a famous example of the dramatic monologue. The speaker of this poem is the wealthy Duke showing off a painting of his former wife. Throughout the poem, he talks about the Duchess, intending to paint a picture of what she was like. However, without meaning to, the Duke actually reveals more about his own character. The reader soon becomes aware that the Duke is a manipulative, untrustworthy speaker with a terrible secret to hide. Faced with this unreliable speaker, the reader must piece together clues to come up with an accurate portrait of the Duchess—and what may have happened to her.

MY LAST DUCHESS
BY ROBERT BROWNING

FERRARA[1]

That's my last Duchess painted on the wall,

Looking as if she were alive. I call

That piece a wonder, now; Frà Pandolf's[2] hands

Worked busily a day, and there she stands.

Will't please you sit and look at her? I said

"Frà Pandolf" by design, for never read

Strangers like you that pictured countenance,[3]

The depth and passion of its earnest glance,

But to myself they turned (since none puts by

The curtain I have drawn for you, but I)

And seemed as they would ask me, if they durst,

How such a glance came there; so, not the first

Are you to turn and ask thus. Sir, 'twas not

Her husband's presence only, called that spot

Of joy into the Duchess' cheek; perhaps

Frà Pandolf chanced to say, "Her mantle laps

Over my lady's wrist too much," or "Paint

Must never hope to reproduce the faint

Half-flush that dies along her throat." Such stuff

Was courtesy, she thought, and cause enough

For calling up that spot of joy. She had

A heart——how shall I say?—— too soon made glad,

Too easily impressed; she liked whate'er

She looked on, and her looks went everywhere.

Sir, 'twas all one! My favor at her breast,[4]

The dropping of the daylight in the West,

The bough of cherries some officious fool

Broke in the orchard for her, the white mule

She rode with round the terrace—all and each

Would draw from her alike the approving speech,

Or blush, at least. She thanked men—good! but thanked

Somehow—I know not how—as if she ranked

My gift of a nine-hundred-years-old name

With anybody's gift. Who'd stoop to blame

This sort of trifling? Even had you skill

In speech—which I have not—to make your will

Quite clear to such an one, and say, "Just this

Or that in you disgusts me; here you miss,

Or there exceed the mark"—and if she let

Herself be lessoned so, nor plainly set

Her wits to yours, forsooth, and made excuse—

E'en then would be some stooping; and I choose

Never to stoop. Oh, sir, she smiled, no doubt,

Whene'er I passed her; but who passed without

Much the same smile? This grew; I gave commands;

Then all smiles stopped together. There she stands

As if alive. Will't please you rise? We'll meet

The company below, then. I repeat,

The Count your master's known munificence

Is ample warrant that no just pretense

Of mine for dowry will be disallowed;

Though his fair daughter's self, as I avowed

At starting, is my object. Nay, we'll go

Together down, sir. Notice Neptune, though,

Taming a sea-horse, thought a rarity,

Which Claus of Innsbruck[5] cast in bronze for me![1]

---

1. Ferrara. Refers to the fifth Duke of Ferrara, an Italian nobleman on whom the character is based

2. Frà Pandolf. Friar Pandolf, a fictional artist

3. Countenance. Face

4. My favor at her breast. A token of favor, such as a ribbon, worn pinned to the clothing as a sign of love

5. Claus of Innsbruck. A fictional sculptor

Summary and Analysis

The poem is composed in heroic couplets, which are rhymed pairs of lines in iambic pentameter. Each line has approximately five pairs of stressed and unstressed syllables: "That's *my* | last *duch* | ess *paint* | ed *on* | the *wall*." Browning uses the technique of enjambment. Because of the enjambment, the rhymes are not as noticeable as in some lyric poetry. The even rhythm and run-on lines give the feeling of natural speech, making it perfect for a dramatic monologue.

As the poem opens, the Duke invites a guest to view a painting of his "last Duchess." The Duke keeps this portrait of his former wife behind a curtain that only he himself is allowed to open. He mentions the name of the portrait painter, Frà Pandolf, as if to impress his listener. The Duke remarks on how lifelike the painting is, and says many strangers are curious about the passionate, earnest look on the Duchess's face.

After inviting his visitor to sit down and look at the painting, the Duke begins to talk about the Duchess. In lines 13–30, he describes her in terms that throw suspicion on her character. According to the Duke, she was a flirtatious person who smiled at everyone, not only her husband. A flattering comment from her

In an age before photography, painted portraits were common among upper-class people.

portrait painter could cause a happy blush, or "spot of joy," to appear on her cheek. She loved everything she saw. Simple pleasures such as a sunset, a bunch of cherries from the orchard, or her pet mule made her just as glad as any gift the Duke could give her. In short, he complains, she was "too soon made glad / Too easily impressed." He feels she did not properly appreciate him and his "gift of a nine-hundred-years-old name."

In lines 34–42, the Duke admits he could have spoken to his wife about her behavior and "lessoned" her to obey his will. However, he claims, he did not have the skill in speech to explain to her exactly what it was that bothered him. Besides, to bring up such "trifling," or silly, issues would have meant "stooping," or lowering himself—something the Duke chooses never to do.

His recounting of his life with his former wife ends in lines 45–46, when the Duke explains, "I gave commands; / Then all smiles stopped together." The statement is ominous, but readers are left with a mystery. What exactly happened to the Duchess?

In line 47, the Duke finishes his story and asks his listener to rise. The next few lines reveal that the Duke's guest is a servant of a neighboring count. The Duke plans to marry the count's daughter, and expects a large

The poem's final image is of a bronze statue of Neptune, the Roman god of the sea.

dowry, or financial reward. As the men leave, the Duke points out another piece of art in his collection—a statue of the god Neptune taming a seahorse.

5

A CHILLING CHARACTER

Robert Browning's dramatic monologue "My Last Duchess" can be analyzed from the point of view of reader response. This type of analysis examines how the structure and content of a poem affect how the reader interprets the work and its meaning. Because of the unreliable narrator, the reader must become like a detective in a murder mystery, using inference and guesswork to form a true picture of the ill-fated Duchess. Even by the end of the monologue, the truth behind the Duke's words remains ambiguous. But the information he shares and the tone he takes paint an ominous picture. The effect of the poem is chilling. The reader experiences a

A reader response analysis studies how the reader interprets the work.

THESIS STATEMENT

The last sentence of the first paragraph is this essay's thesis statement. It reads: "The reader experiences a growing sense of horror and irony as the Duke, seeking to blame his wife, unwittingly reveals his jealous, possessive, and perhaps even murderous nature." This essay will focus on the reader's emotional reactions throughout the poem.

ARGUMENT ONE

The author introduces her first argument: "As the monologue begins, the Duke seems to speak directly to the reader, drawing the reader into the story." In this paragraph, the author will support the thesis by explaining how the first part of the poem draws readers into the mystery.

growing sense of horror and irony as the Duke, seeking to blame his wife, unwittingly reveals his jealous, possessive, and perhaps even murderous nature.

As the monologue begins, the Duke seems to speak directly to the reader, drawing the reader into the story. The curtain drawn back, he announces: "That's my last Duchess painted on the wall, / Looking as if she were alive." Through his description, the reader envisions a beautiful young woman with rosy cheeks and bright eyes. What happened to the Duchess? The Duke's wording makes it unclear. He could simply mean the painting is very lifelike, or he could be implying she is dead. The wording is intentionally unclear, leaving the reader with a sense of mystery and intrigue.

At first, the Duke leads the reader to see the Duchess in a negative light. **Pointing** out the passionate expression on her face, he notes: "'twas not / Her husband's presence only, called that spot / Of joy into the Duchess's cheek." His description of the conversation between the Duchess and the painter suggests they were flirtatious, or perhaps even in love. The reader wonders: Did the Duke catch his wife in an affair?

As the Duke continues his monologue, the reader finds clues that his story is unreliable. **He** claims "her looks went everywhere"—implying she had an eye for other men. Yet the examples of things the Duchess loved—a sunset, some cherries from the orchard, and a white mule—are so wholesome and pure as to paint the Duchess as one who simply savors life and the Duke as unreasonably jealous. Her implied affair with the portrait artist also seems unlikely, since the

ARGUMENT TWO

The author introduces her second argument: "At first, the Duke leads the reader to see the Duchess in a negative light."

ARGUMENT THREE

In the third argument, the author explains how the reader's reaction changes: "As the Duke continues his monologue, the reader finds clues that his story is unreliable."

artist, Frà Pandolf, was a friar, a man under holy orders. Browning may have purposely included this detail as a clue to readers that there was no affair between the artist and the Duchess—it was all in the Duke's jealous imagination.

Ironically, although the Duke intends to create an unflattering depiction of his wife, the reader instead sees the negative side of his character. The Duke is a prideful man who believes his "nine-hundred-years-old-name" makes him superior to others. He refuses to "stoop," or lower himself, even to his wife. The Duke expected his wife to show gratitude when he married her, since he gave her the "gift" of high social status. In contrast, the Duchess was a simple, unpretentious person who treated everyone as her equal. Her refusal to honor his rank and title inflamed the Duke with jealous rage.

The more the Duke rambles, the more the reader suspects him—until at last he seems to confess to

ARGUMENT FOUR
The author introduces her fourth argument: "Ironically, although the Duke intends to create an unflattering depiction of his wife, the reader instead sees the negative side of his character." This paragraph goes on to describe the reader's negative impressions of the Duke

The character of the Duke thinks highly of his own elevated social status.

ARGUMENT FIVE

The author continues to describe
the reader's reaction to the Duke
in this paragraph. "The more
the Duke rambles, the more the
reader suspects him—until at
last he seems to confess to a
terrible crime."

a terrible crime. He refers to his concerns as "trifling," or silly, yet he clearly takes them seriously. He claims he had no "skill / In speech" to make his wife understand his feelings, yet his entire speech is evidence that he is actually very eloquent. The Duke wants his listeners to think he was a helpless, wronged husband, harmed by his wife's unfaithfulness. Instead, readers realize he was actually a tyrannical, possessive husband who could not bear to see his wife smile at anyone but him. At last, he says, "I gave commands; / Then all smiles stopped together." This chilling statement sounds like a confession of murder, yet it comes as such a casual remark that it leaves the reader to wonder. How did the smiles stop? Could he have had his wife killed?

The reader's shock turns to dread as Browning reveals the last bit of information: the Duke is about to be married again. Only now

ARGUMENT SIX

In this argument, the author
describes the reader's reaction
of dread near the end of the
poem. "The reader's shock turns
to dread as Browning reveals the
last bit of information: the Duke is
about to be married again."

The reader is left with the impression that the Duke may make his next wife simply another object in his collection of luxuries.

does Browning reveal the identity of the Duke's visitor, an emissary of the Count, and their business, which is to arrange the Duke's marriage to the Count's daughter. The Duke asks first about the generous dowry he expects to receive from his new bride, making it obvious that his interest in her is due to money, not love. She will be just another possession to him, like the objects of art he is so proud to show off.

ARGUMENT SEVEN

In the final argument, the author describes evidence for the notion that the Duke's next wife may end up like his previous one. "As the poem ends, the reader is left with the fear that the Duke's second wife, just like the first, may end up just another object in the Duke's collection."

As the poem ends, the reader is left with the fear that the Duke's second wife, just like the first, may end up just another object in the Duke's collection. She could be shut behind a curtain to be viewed only at his pleasure. In the final lines of the poem, the Duke proudly points out another object in his art collection, a bronze sculpture of the god Neptune taming a seahorse. The statue reflects his view of himself as a godlike figure with ultimate control over helpless creatures.

Throughout the poem, the unreliable narrator has given the reader a sense of unease about the truth behind his past. As the reader pieces clues together, the apparent truth becomes clearer and more chilling.

CONCLUSION

The last paragraph of the essay is the conclusion. The author summarizes the reader's reaction to the poem, which was introduced in her thesis.

By the end of the work, it seems clear the Duke was likely behind his wife's disappearance, and that his future wife may fall victim to the same fate.

THINKING
CRITICALLY

Now it's your turn to assess the essay. Consider these questions:

1. According to the author, what emotional responses do readers have to "My Last Duchess" and why? Does the author do a good job of describing a typical reader's reaction? How did you react when you read the poem?

2. Do you agree with the author's interpretation of the poem? Which part of the essay did you find most interesting? Were there any points you disagreed with? Explain.

3. Are there any other possible ways to interpret the Duke's words and behavior?

OTHER

APPROACHES

The essay you have just read describes a typical reader's response to the poem "My Last Duchess." Below are two other ways you might approach the poem.

Historical Criticism

Historical criticism attempts to examine a work of literature with reference to its historical context. Although Browning's poem was written in the 1840s in Victorian England, details in the poem suggest it is set in the Italian Renaissance. The main character may have been inspired by a real-life Duke of Ferrara, Alfonso II d'Este, the fifth Duke of Ferrara (1533–1598). The Duke's first wife, Lucrezia De' Medici, died at age 16 after only two years of marriage, leading to rumors she was poisoned. Browning may have found this antique murder mystery an interesting premise for his poem. A possible thesis statement from the angle of historical criticism might be: Browning's poem "My Last Duchess" reflects Victorian writers' fascination with the characters and settings of the Italian Renaissance.

Gender Criticism

Gender criticism explores how gender relationships are represented in a work of literature. "My Last Duchess" has been examined by feminist critics who view the Duke as a stereotypical male chauvinist—a man who believes he is superior to women. Rather than treating his wife as an equal, the Duke wished to dominate her completely. He did not want the Duchess to have interests or desires of her own. Instead, he wanted to keep her and her smiles all to himself, as if she were an object or possession. A possible thesis statement that examines the poem from this viewpoint might be: The poem "My Last Duchess" depicts a gender relationship in which a man desires absolute power over women, viewing them as objects to be possessed.

6

OVERVIEWS OF
TWO ELEGIES

An elegy is a poem of serious reflection on the theme of death, often expressing a lament for someone who has died. The tone of an elegy is typically somber and sorrowful. Elegies originated in ancient Greece. Traditionally, they contained three stanzas: first a lament, expressing grief for the lost loved one; then praise for the person who died; and finally, consolation.

Poet Emily Dickinson (1830–1886) is known for her poems about death and mortality. Born in Amherst, Massachusetts, she spent most of her adult life in her home, rarely venturing out or entertaining visitors. However, her correspondence and writing show her lively wit and fearless poetic sensibility. When she died, she left behind hundreds of unpublished poems, finally

Emily Dickinson became famous as a poet
only after her death.

becoming known as one of the most noted poetic voices in the United States.

Critics often describe Dickinson as being a poet ahead of her time. Her poems have an unconventional form. They include dashes, line breaks, slant rhyme, and capitalization. Her poem "Because I could not stop for Death" is a good example. Not only does it contain unusual capitalization and punctuation, it takes a unique view of a typically somber topic. Although some might categorize the poem as an elegy, it lacks the expected elements of grief, praise, and consolation. Instead, Dickinson's poem takes the reader on an imagined journey toward eternity. Her poem is a contemplation of the afterlife.

Dickinson's well-known poem can be contrasted with another unconventional elegy by Japanese-American writer Yuko Taniguchi. Taniguchi was born in Yokohama, Japan, in 1975 and moved to the United States as a teenager. She teaches writing at the University of Minnesota in Rochester and has written the poetry collection *Foreign Wife Elegy,* published in 2004. In the title poem, Taniguchi describes the moment of a woman's death from her own point of view.

Both Dickinson and Taniguchi focus on the theme of death.

BECAUSE I COULD NOT STOP FOR DEATH
EMILY DICKINSON

Because I could not stop for Death —
He kindly stopped for me —
The Carriage held but just Ourselves —
And Immortality.

We slowly drove — He knew no haste
And I had put away
My labor and my leisure too,
For His Civility —

We passed the School, where Children strove
At Recess — in the Ring —
We passed the Fields of Gazing Grain —
We passed the Setting Sun —

Or rather — He passed us —
The Dews drew quivering and chill —
For only Gossamer, my Gown —
My Tippet — only Tulle —

We paused before a House that seemed

A Swelling of the Ground —

The Roof was scarcely visible —

The Cornice — in the Ground —

Since then — 'tis Centuries — and yet

Feels shorter than the Day

I first surmised the Horses' Heads

Were toward Eternity —[1]

———————————

FOREIGN WIFE ELEGY
YUKO TANIGUCHI

My language has its own world

where he doesn't know how to live,

but he should learn my language;

then he can call my mother to say

that I am dead. I drive too fast

and someone else drives too fast

and we crash on the icy road.

The death sweeps me away.

He can tell this to my mother

if he learns my language.

Her large yellow voice travels

and hits his body, but at least she knows

that I am dead, and if I die,

I want him to tell my mother

with his deep voice shaking.[2]

Summary and Analysis

Dickinson's poem is an allegory, or extended metaphor, comparing Death to a leisurely carriage ride. Death is personified as a polite gentleman suitor. He "kindly" stops by to take the speaker for a ride in his horse-drawn carriage, accompanied by Immortality. The three of them ride along slowly, passing schoolchildren at play, fields of grain, and the setting sun. Soon, the speaker begins to feel chilly, as she is wearing only a sheer gown and a shawl of light netting. At last, the carriage pauses near a house that seems to be only a swelling of the ground, with its roof scarcely showing. This is the speaker's grave. In the final stanza, it is revealed that the speaker has now been dead for "Centuries"; the poem has all along been narrated by a dead person.

In Taniguchi's poem, the speaker is a "foreign wife" whose husband does not speak her native tongue. She wants him to learn her language so that if she dies, he will be able to inform her mother. She envisions her own death in a car crash on an icy road, described in lines 5–8. After death "sweeps" her away, she envisions her husband calling her mother to deliver the terrible news. Taniguchi references stereotypes about East Asian people when she imagines that the mother's voice will sound

Taniguchi's speaker imagines what might happen if she dies in a car crash on a wintry road.

"large" and "yellow" to the speaker's husband. Still, the mother's grief "hits" the husband, leaving him "with his deep voice shaking."

ELEGIES AND GENRE CRITICISM

Genre criticism involves studying how a work fits with the normal conventions of its genre. A genre is a particular style or format of poetry or prose that shares certain characteristics. Genre criticism can show how a work conforms to or departs from traditional genre conventions, and it can suggest how this affects the interpretation of the work.

One common poetic genre is the elegy, which deals with the theme of death. Both Dickinson and Taniguchi describe the moment of a woman's death from her own

A gloomy, sad tone is a common element of the elegy genre.

point of view. But despite this similarity, a genre analysis shows that Dickinson's "Because I could not stop for Death" and Taniguchi's "Foreign Wife Elegy" use the elegy for different purposes. Dickinson imagines death as a peaceful journey toward eternity, while Taniguchi depicts the stark grief of the loved ones left behind, emphasizing the human need to be remembered after death.

Dickinson's poem provides a strikingly unconventional depiction of death. Rather than seeing Death as cruel or frightening, the speaker calls him "kindly" and remarks on his "Civility." She seems to welcome his unexpected visit. Death is doing her a favor by stopping for her, since, like most people, she was so

THESIS STATEMENT

The last sentence of the first paragraph is this essay's thesis statement. It reads: "Dickinson imagines death as a peaceful journey toward eternity, while Taniguchi depicts the stark grief of the loved ones left behind, emphasizing the human need to be remembered after death." This essay will compare and contrast how the two poems treat the theme of death.

ARGUMENT ONE

The author introduces her first argument: "Dickinson's poem provides a strikingly unconventional depiction of death." In the next three paragraphs, the author will explain how the poem's treatment of death is unusual.

occupied with worldly duties that she had no time to stop for him.

As she makes her journey toward the grave, the speaker looks back on her life without the usual sentimentality or sorrow. The ride is slow and peaceful as they pass a school, autumn fields, and finally the setting sun. As described by critic Charles M. Anderson, these all stand for stages of the speaker's life, "youth, maturity, and age," and

A sunset is one of the images Dickinson evokes in her poem.

also the "the natural route of a funeral train, past the schoolhouse to the village, then the outlying fields, and on to the remote burying ground."[1] The ride to her final resting place is compared to the homecoming of a bride. The speaker is wearing gossamer and tulle, a typical bridal outfit, and the grave is described as if it were a cozy home.

The tone of the poem is unusual for an elegy, as it lacks the conventional elements of grief and consolation. In her biography of Emily Dickinson, Cynthia Griffin Wolff calls the poem an "astonishing narrative" made even more remarkable by the speaker's "steady, unruffled tone."[2] The speaker accepts her death calmly, without grief, even though the eternity she looked forward to is no consolation, but instead an eerie, unending stretch of nothingness. In the end, however, Wolff sees the poem as triumphant, a testimony to "the poet's victory over time and mortality."[3] The speaker, and Dickinson herself, will live on forever through the words of the poem.

Dickinson imagines death as a somber carriage ride.

ARGUMENT FOUR

The fourth argument provides a transition to the second poem being discussed. Here the author makes a connection between Taniguchi's poem and Dickinson's: "Taniguchi's poem uses the present tense to give the impression the speaker is actually dead."

Taniguchi's poem uses the present tense to give the impression the speaker is actually dead. Like Dickinson, Taniguchi also depicts the moment of a person's death as seen through her own eyes. The speaker imagines dying in a car crash: "I drive too fast / and someone else drives too fast / and we crash on the icy road. / The death sweeps me away." The phrase "I am dead" occurs twice, once in line 5 and again in line 13. In the third-to-last line, however, the speaker includes the words "if I die," making it clear that, unlike Dickinson's speaker, she is talking about an imagined scenario.

ARGUMENT FIVE

In argument five, the author explains how Taniguchi's poem is different from Dickinson's: "Whereas Dickinson depicts the journey toward eternity, Taniguchi instead focuses on the people left behind."

Whereas Dickinson depicts the journey toward eternity, Taniguchi instead focuses on the people left behind. The speaker yearns for greater understanding between herself and her husband. He does not speak

The speaker worries that due to a cultural divide, her husband's relationship with her mother will differ dramatically from her own.

her language or understand her culture, and therefore, she feels he cannot really know her completely: "My language has its own world / Where he doesn't know how to live." Even her own mother would seem foreign to him, a "yellow" person with a "large" voice. Their conversation would be like a clash of cultures.

ARGUMENT SIX

In this final argument, the author explains the theme of the second poem: "Taniguchi's poem, then, is not about death but about the need for a deeper connection."

Taniguchi's poem, then, is not about death but about the need for a deeper connection. The speaker needs her husband to learn more about her language and culture so he will be able to love her as completely and absolutely as her own mother does. Only then will he be able to grieve her properly when she is gone. Instead of wishing to console her husband, she wants him to be left with his "deep voice shaking." She needs him to feel the full impact of her loss because it is the only evidence of a deep and true understanding.

Both Dickinson and Taniguchi create memorable poems on the theme of death that go beyond the sentimental elegy. Through unexpected comparisons and startling points of view, they invite readers to see

Dickinson and Taniguchi each use the elegy genre to give a fresh perspective on the theme of death.

this theme in a new way. Dickinson's poem reimagines death as a kindly suitor who woos us away from life to a place beyond time, while Taniguchi examines how the prospect of death spurs us toward a deeper connection with the living. Genre criticism of the two works shows that while both authors are using the age-old genre of the elegy, their unconventional elements give each poem a unique, fresh point of view.

CONCLUSION

The last paragraph of the essay is the conclusion. The author restates her main idea, that both poems are unconventional elegies that invite readers to view the theme of death in a new way.

THINKING
CRITICALLY

Now it's your turn to assess the essay. Consider these questions:

1. Do you agree with the author that the two poems convey an unusual view of death?

2. Were there any points in the essay that you disagreed with? Explain.

3. Which poem did you find it easier to visualize? How did the author's use of language accomplish this?

OTHER
APPROACHES

The essay you have just read uses genre criticism to analyze two poems in comparison to a traditional elegy. Below are two other ways you might approach the poem.

Reader Response

Reader response analysis seeks to analyze how the reader's reaction helps create the meaning of the poem. Since poems with the theme of death often have a powerful effect on readers, reader response analysis is a good way to approach elegies. A thesis statement for a reader response analysis could be: Both Dickinson and Taniguchi describe the moment of a woman's death from her own point of view, forcing readers to confront their own fears of mortality.

Rhetorical Analysis: Poetic Technique

Poets employ rhetorical techniques such as rhyme, meter, and figurative language to create a particular effect on the reader.

To analyze a poem's rhetorical techniques, you can scan the lines to determine the meter, mark the rhyme scheme, and identify examples of simile and metaphor. Dickinson's poem is written in rhyming quatrains of iambic tetrameter. Many of the rhymes are not exact, but in general, the rhyme scheme of each quatrain is *abcb*. There are eight syllables per line, with the stress falling on every other syllable. The rhyme and meter echo the form and mood of a hymn, a religious song of praise often sung in a church. The poem also contains numerous examples of alliteration, or repeated consonant sounds at the beginnings of words, as in "labor" and "leisure"; "Recess" and "Ring"; "Gazing Grain"; "Setting Sun"; "Gossamer" and "Gown"; and "Tippet" and "Tulle." The repeated sounds add to the musical effect of the poem. A possible thesis that examines Dickinson's poem through the lens of rhetorical technique might be: Dickinson uses rhyme, meter, and sound techniques to give her poem about death the solemn, mesmerizing effect of a hymn.

8

OVERVIEWS OF "DREAM VARIATIONS" AND "FANTASY"

The Harlem Renaissance was a time of great cultural, literary, and artistic flowering in the African-American community. It took place across the United States, but was especially centered in New York City, in the African-American neighborhood of Harlem. The movement began in the 1920s as thousands of blacks moved north in search of a better way of life. Black poets, writers, artists, musicians, and dancers gathered in the northern cities. Their work expressed a new pride in African-American culture and heritage.

Langston Hughes (1902–1967) was one of the best-known poets of the Harlem Renaissance. Born in

Langston Hughes spent time in Africa, Europe, and Mexico.

Missouri, he moved to Harlem as a young man in 1921 and joined the literary community. In his poetry and other writing, he strove to be a voice of the people, describing the everyday lives of working-class African Americans and their struggles and dreams. His poetry

Composer and bandleader Duke Ellington, *left*, was a major musical figure in the Harlem Renaissance.

shows the influence of jazz and blues music, which he considered uniquely African-American art forms.

Hughes's poetry was influenced by his interest in Africa. He visited Africa in 1923. In his autobiography, he describes his first impression of Africa: "A long sandy coastline, gleaming in the sun. Palm trees sky-tall. . . . People black and beautiful as the night."[1] This imagery is echoed in the poem "Dream Variations," in which Hughes describes a "tall, slim tree" and compares himself to the blackness of night.

Gwendolyn Bennett (1902–1981) was a painter and illustrator as well as a poet, fiction writer, and teacher. She attended Columbia University and joined Harlem's community of writers along with Hughes. Her poems celebrate the beauty and dignity of African-American women.

During the 1920s, both Hughes and Bennett published many poems in leading African-American magazines, making them important voices of their time. Their poems "Dream Variations" (1924) and "Fantasy" (1927) use vivid images of color and movement to share dreams of African-American freedom.

FANTASY
BY GWENDOLYN BENNETT

I sailed in my dreams to the Land of Night
Where you were the dusk-eyed queen,
And there in the pallor of moon-veiled light
The loveliest things were seen . . .

A slim-necked peacock sauntered there
In a garden of lavender hues,
And you were strange with your purple hair
As you sat in your amethyst chair
With your feet in your hyacinth shoes.

Oh, the moon gave a bluish light
Through the trees in the land of dreams and night.
I stood behind a bush of yellow-green
And whistled a song to the dark-haired queen . . . [2]

Bennett evokes images of brilliant colors, including those in a peacock's plumage.

The image of a tall, slim tree in the night recurs
in Hughes' poem.

To fling my arms wide

In some place of the sun,

To whirl and to dance

Till the white day is done.

Then rest at cool evening

Beneath a tall tree

While night comes on gently,

Dark like me—

That is my dream!

To fling my arms wide

In the face of the sun,

Dance! Whirl! Whirl!

Till the quick day is done.

Rest at pale evening . . .

A tall, slim tree . . .

Night coming tenderly

Black like me. [3]

Summary and Analysis

Bennett's poem "Fantasy" is an example of Imagism, a style of modernist poetry that aims to create a single vivid image. In the poem, the speaker shares her dream of traveling to the "Land of Night." By the light of the moon, she sees a dark-eyed queen seated in a "garden of lavender hues." The queen's chair, shoes, and hair are colored in shades of purple. A peacock saunters in the garden and the moon gives a "bluish light." The speaker hides behind a bush of "yellow-green" and whistles a song to the queen.

Langston Hughes's poem "Dream Variations" is written in the style of theme and variation, common in blues and jazz music. The second stanza is a variation of the first, repeating the same ideas but with a few changes in wording. In the poem, the speaker describes his dream. He longs to fling his arms wide in the sun, dancing and whirling until the "white day" or "quick day" is done. He will rest in the evening as the night comes on "gently" and "tenderly." Night is like himself—"Dark like me," and "Black like me."

The color purple is a recurring theme in "Fantasy."

9

A HISTORICAL ANALYSIS

Historical analysis involves studying a work in the context of the events that were happening around the time when it was written. This lens examines what authors may have been doing or thinking while creating their works, and it suggests how this historical context may have affected the work itself.

The poetry of the Harlem Renaissance contains powerful messages about African-American identity. These messages can be best understood in the context of their historical moment. Since the time of slavery, African Americans had been taught that their dark skin made them

Hughes, *right*, grew up in Kansas in the early 1900s and wrote about the reality of life as an African American within his own historical context.

inferior to white people and that Africa was a savage place without enlightenment. Poets such as Hughes and Bennett helped create a new and positive self-image for African-American people.

In their poems, images of darkness and night have a symbolic meaning, representing the beauty and dignity of African-American people in a time of racial inequality.

During the Harlem Renaissance, writers looked to their African heritage as a source of identity, finding nobility in the history of African nations. In her poem "Fantasy," Bennett describes a dream image of an African queen. Vivid colors abound in the poem, in stark contrast to a racist world of black and white. The queen is surrounded by the color purple, the traditional color of royalty. Her throne is

THESIS STATEMENT

The author states her thesis in the last sentence of the first paragraph: "In their poems, images of darkness and night have a symbolic meaning, representing the beauty and dignity of African-American people in a time of racial inequality."

ARGUMENT ONE

In her first argument, the author focuses on how poets of the time looked to their African heritage as a source of identity. The first argument is: "During the Harlem Renaissance, writers looked to their African heritage as a source of identity, finding nobility in the history of African nations."

"amethyst," her shoes are "hyacinth," and even her hair is purple. A peacock struts nearby, representing the queen's beauty and pride. A bush has the "yellow-green" color of springtime, perhaps symbolizing a new beginning for African Americans, the spring of a new era. The queen is described as "dusk-eyed" and "dark-haired," emphasizing her dark beauty, and Africa is described in a positive way as a "land of dreams and night."

Beautiful, dark, glittering, and mysterious, night for Bennett was a symbol of the beauty and power of African-American women, who were not valued or appreciated in the white-dominated American culture. According to critic Nina Miller, this image of a "nightwoman" was common in Harlem Renaissance poetry.[1] Black Americans were no longer enslaved after the Civil War (1861–1865), but by the 1920s and 1930s, they still did not enjoy equal rights or respect. Writing about the beauty of night was

ARGUMENT TWO

In her second argument, the author explains the symbolic meaning of night in Bennett's poetry. The second argument is: "Beautiful, dark, glittering, and mysterious, night for Bennett was a symbol of the beauty and power of African-American women, who were not valued or appreciated in the white-dominated American culture."

a way for black poets to show, in the words of scholar Maureen Honey, "the primacy of Blackness in a world that favored white things."[2]

Besides its dark beauty, night also represented freedom from the white world. Since the majority of employers were white, most African Americans spent the working day being supervised by white bosses. They could not talk openly about their feelings or dreams, and often felt they had to hide their true selves to survive. Only at night, when they joined their friends and family, were they free from racist judgment. In Bennett's poem, the queen is viewed in "moon-veiled light." This reference to a veil suggests that the night protects her from judging eyes. As explained by Honey, the nightwoman of Bennett's poetry is "a goddess whose features are hidden. . . . Although night is veiled in mystery, she escapes the distorted, negative images of those who fail to see her clearly."[3]

Hughes's poem "Dream Variations" also contains positive imagery of Africa. The "place of the sun" where the speaker dreams of whirling and dancing can be interpreted as a place in Africa, the homeland of his people, where he dreams of returning. In this interpretation, the "tall, slim tree" could be seen as a palm tree, a common sight on African shores. During the 1920s, a "Back to Africa" movement was being led by publisher and journalist Marcus Garvey. Many African Americans felt that returning to Africa was the only way to escape, once and for all, the evils of oppression. Hughes traveled to Africa in 1923, one year before he first published "Dream Variations."

Similar to Bennett, Hughes describes night and darkness in positive terms, using them to represent African-American culture and freedom. The speaker

ARGUMENT FOUR

In her fourth argument, the author explains how Hughes's poem is similar to Bennett's in its portrayal of Africa. The argument states: "Hughes's poem 'Dream Variations' also contains positive imagery of Africa."

ARGUMENT FIVE

The fifth and final argument of the essay explains how Hughes, like Bennett, uses darkness and night symbolically. The argument states: "Similar to Bennett, Hughes describes night and darkness in positive terms, using them to represent African-American culture and freedom."

Garvey promoted the return to Africa by people of African ancestry

talks of night as coming "gently" and "tenderly," in contrast with the day, which is "white" and "quick." The term "quick" seems to refer to the workaday world, in which everyone is busy and on a schedule. Night, meaning African culture, is more relaxed and connected with nature, as shown in the image of a speaker resting beneath a tree. Night, too, is like the speaker himself—"Dark like me," and "Black like me." It is a time when a black man can feel comfortable; he can be himself. The poem can be understood on several levels. On one level, the poem is simply about a man's desire to get through the workday so he can relax and have fun at night. The day is "white" because it is light outside. But understood in the context of the times, the "white day" can be seen to represent the oppressive environment of a white-dominated world. The speaker longs to enjoy a "place in the sun," but all such positions of advantage are taken by whites. He longs to break free from their control, dancing and whirling until "the white day is done." Only then, when the white power has dimmed to pale evening, can he begin to stretch upward to greater heights, like the "tall, slim tree."

As did other poets and writers of the Harlem Renaissance, Hughes and Bennett used beautiful imagery of darkness and night to contradict the racist attitude of white superiority and assert African-American worth and pride. These young writers refused to accept the idea of Africa as a savage, uncivilized place, as their ancestors had been taught during the times of slavery. Their poems show pride in their African heritage. To these poets, their African homeland symbolized hope for freedom. It was a "land of dreams" and a "place of the sun" where dark-skinned people could have value and dignity, free from a white-ruled world.

CONCLUSION

The last paragraph of this essay serves as the conclusion. It restates the ideas that have been argued throughout the essay, that Hughes and Bennett used images of darkness and night to assert African-American worth and pride

THINKING CRITICALLY

Now it's your turn to assess the essay. Consider these questions:

1. Which is the strongest argument in the essay? Why?

2. Do you agree with the author's interpretation of the colors in Bennett's poem? What other interpretations might be possible?

3. The author states that Hughes's poem can be understood on several levels. What was your understanding of the poem when you first read it? Did your interpretation change after reading the essay? Explain.

4. Is it necessary that readers understand the historical context of the Harlem Renaissance in order to appreciate the poems? Why or why not?

OTHER

APPROACHES

The previous essay examines the poems in light of their historical context. The poems might be analyzed in different ways. For example, an essay could focus on the poems' use of rhyme and meter to create an effect. Another approach might analyze the poems using biographical information about each poet.

Formal Criticism: Rhyme, Rhythm, and Meaning

Analyzing a poem based on its literary techniques, such as rhyme and meter, can bring a new understanding of the poet's craft. Such an analysis of a poem's form is known as formal criticism. An analysis of "Dream Variations" might describe the type of meter used and how it contributes to a feeling of movement and contrast. Longer lines with a slower rhythm create an easygoing mood, while the shorter lines are stern and severe, emphasizing the harshness of the "white day." A thesis statement that uses this approach could be: Hughes uses rhythm in his poem to emphasize the contrasts between the black and white worlds.

Biographical Criticism

Biographical criticism seeks to interpret a literary work by relating it to the writer's life and experiences. Similar to other artists and writers of the Harlem Renaissance, Hughes and Bennett were personally concerned with black pride and identity in a white-dominated society. As Hughes put it, they intended "to express our individual dark-skinned selves without fear or shame."[4] Learning more about the lives of these poets can help readers better understand their poems. A thesis statement that uses biographical criticism to analyze both poems might be: Hughes and Bennett expressed their personal beliefs and dreams through their poetry.

ANALYZE IT!

Now that you have learned different approaches to analyzing a work, are you ready to perform your own analysis? You have read that this type of evaluation can help you look at literature in a new way and make you pay attention to certain issues you may not have otherwise recognized. So, why not use one of these approaches to consider a fresh take on your favorite work?

First, choose a philosophy, critical theory, or other approach and consider which work or works you want to analyze. Remember the approach you choose is a springboard for asking questions about the works.

Next, write a specific question that relates to your approach or philosophy. Then you can form your thesis, which should provide the answer to that question. Your thesis is the most important part of your analysis and offers an argument about the work, considering its characters, plot, or literary techniques, or what it says about society or the world. Recall that the thesis statement typically appears at the very end of the introductory paragraph of your essay. It is usually only one sentence long.

After you have written your thesis, find evidence to back it up. Good places to start are in the work itself or in journals or articles that discuss what other people have said about it. You may also want to read about the author or creator's life so you can get a sense of what factors may have affected the creative process. This can be especially useful if you are considering how the work connects to history or the author's intent.

You should also explore parts of the book that seem to disprove your thesis and create an argument against them. As you do this, you might want to address what others have written about the book. Their quotes may help support your claim.

Before you start analyzing a work, think about the different arguments made in this book. Reflect on how evidence supporting the thesis was presented. Did you find that some of the techniques used to back up the arguments were more convincing than others? Try these methods as you prove your thesis in your own analysis paper.

When you are finished writing your analysis, read it over carefully. Is your thesis statement understandable? Do the supporting arguments flow logically, with the topic of each paragraph clearly stated? Can you add any information that would present your readers with a stronger argument in favor of your thesis? Were you able to use quotes from the book, as well as from other critics, to enhance your ideas?

Did you see the work in a new light?

GLOSSARY

ALLUSION
A reference to something well known, such as a person, event, or work of literature.

CLICHÉ
An overused word or expression.

CYNICAL
Having a negative and distrustful view.

DRAMATIC MONOLOGUE
A poem written in the form of a speech.

HYACINTH
A sweet-smelling flower that appears in a variety of colors, including purple.

METAPHOR
A figure of speech that compares two objects or ideas.

METER
A poem's rhythmical pattern, or combination of stressed and unstressed syllables.

OCTAVE
An eight-line stanza.

PARODY
A piece of writing that imitates another work with the purpose of mocking or poking fun at the original author's message.

QUATRAIN
A six-line stanza.

SESTET
A six-line stanza.

SYMBOL
Something, such as an image or idea, that may also represent something else.

ADDITIONAL
RESOURCES

SELECTED BIBLIOGRAPHY

Booth, Stephen, ed. *Shakespeare's Sonnets.* New Haven, CT: Yale UP, 2000. Print.

Charters, Ann, and Samuel Charters, eds. *Literature and Its Writers.* Boston, MA: Bedford/St. Martin's, 2013. Print.

Gates, Henry Louis, Jr., and Valerie A. Smith, eds. *The Norton Anthology of African American Literature, Third Edition.* New York: Norton, 2014. Print.

Wolf, Cynthia Griffin. *Emily Dickinson.* New York: Knopf, 1986. Print.

FURTHER READINGS

Carper, Thomas, and Derek Attridge. *Meter and Meaning: An Introduction to Rhythm in Poetry.* New York: Routledge, 2003. Print.

Combs, Maggie. *Love.* Minneapolis, MN: Abdo, 2016. Print.

Kesselring, Mari. *How to Analyze the Works of William Shakespeare.* Minneapolis, MN: Abdo, 2013. Print.

WEBSITES

To learn more about Essential Literary Genres, visit **booklinks.abdopublishing.com**. These links are routinely monitored and updated to provide the most current information available.

FOR MORE INFORMATION

For more information on this subject, contact or visit the following organizations:

The American Poetry Museum
716 Monroe Street NE, Studio #25
Washington, DC 20017
http://www.americanpoetrymuseum.org
The American Poetry Museum is one of the first museums in the United States dedicated to the study of poetry. The museum exhibits objects relating to American poetry and hosts poetry writing workshops and other events.

The Browning Society
http://www.browningsociety.org
The Browning Society organizes lectures and events to promote the poetry of Robert and Elizabeth Barrett Browning. The group is helping support the restoration of Casa Guidi, the Brownings' home in Florence, Italy. Membership is open to anyone interested in the Brownings' poetry.

Emily Dickinson Museum
280 Main Street
Amherst, MA 01002
http://www.emilydickinsonmuseum.org
Visitors to the Emily Dickinson Museum can explore the house where Dickinson grew up and lived most of her life, along with the home of her brother and his family. Both are located on a three-acre lot in Amherst, Massachusetts. The museum's website also contains links and resources about the poet's life and work.

SOURCE NOTES

CHAPTER 1. INTRODUCTION TO LITERARY GENRES
None.

CHAPTER 2. OVERVIEWS OF SONNET 130 AND 'LOVE SONG FOR LOVE SONGS'
1. William Shakespeare. "Sonnet 130." *Poets.org*. Academy of American Poets, n.d. Web. 1 Aug. 2016.
2. Rafael Campo. "Love Song for Love Songs." *Poets.org*. Academy of American Poets, n.d. Web. 1 Aug. 2016.

CHAPTER 3. RHETORICAL ANALYSIS OF LOVE SONNETS
None.

CHAPTER 4. AN OVERVIEW OF 'MY LAST DUCHESS'
1. Robert Browning. "My Last Duchess." *Poetry Foundation*. Poetry Foundation, 2016. Web. 1 Aug. 2016.

CHAPTER 5. A CHILLING CHARACTER
None.

CHAPTER 6. OVERVIEWS OF TWO ELEGIES
1. Emily Dickinson. "Because I could not stop for Death." *Poets.org*. Academy of American Poets, n.d. Web. 1 Aug. 2016.
2. Yuko Taniguchi. "Foreign Wife Elegy." *Poets.org*. Academy of American Poets, n.d. Web. 1 Aug. 2016.

CHAPTER 7. ELEGIES AND GENRE CRITICISM

1. Charles R. Anderson. *Emily Dickinson's Poetry: Stairway of Surprise.* New York: Holt, 1960. Print. 243.

2. Cynthia Griffin Wolf. *Emily Dickinson.* New York: Alfred A. Knopf, 1986. Print. 276.

3. Ibid.

CHAPTER 8. OVERVIEWS OF "DREAM VARIATIONS" AND "FANTASY"

1. Langston Hughes. "Out of Soundings." *Lapham's Quarterly.* Lapham's Quarterly, n.d. Web. 1 Aug. 2016.

2. Gwendolyn Bennett. "Fantasy." *Poets.org.* Academy of American Poets, n.d. Web. 1 Aug. 2016.

3. Langston Hughes. "Dream Variations." *Poets.org.* Academy of American Poets, n.d. Web. 1 Aug. 2016.

CHAPTER 9. A HISTORICAL ANALYSIS

1. "On 'Street Lamps in Early Spring.'" *Modern American Poetry.* University of Illinois, n.d. Web. 1 Aug. 2016.

2. Ibid.

3. Ibid.

4. "Hughes's 'The Negro Artist and the Racial Mountain.'" *Modern American Poetry.* University of Illinois, n.d. Web. 1 Aug. 2016.

INDEX

ABOUT THE AUTHOR

Jennifer Joline Anderson is a writer and editor with a background in educational textbook publishing. She holds a bachelor's degree in Hispanic Studies from Vassar College, and enjoys literature in both English and Spanish. Jennifer has written many books for young people, including a biography of poet Langston Hughes and study guides for Shakespeare's plays. She lives in Minneapolis.